TWINSEPARABLE

The Untold Story Of Fraternals

Anita Brown, Esq.

DEDICATION

Obviously, I dedicate this book primarily to my twin sister, Audrey Hazel Brown-Givens. Suffice it to say, she is my world. It may be a twin thing, or maybe our bond goes even beyond that, but I don't know what I would do without her in my life. She is my sequel, so to speak, and I her prequel. Even I am tickled silly that I have this life partner who knows me like no other, loves me like no other and has had my back, literally since the womb.

I also dedicate this book to all twins. Twins rock. They rule. It's that simple. I'm just stating the facts, folks. We can't help it. We didn't ask for this duality, but we might as well enjoy it while we can. Teehee.

Copyright © 2016 Anita Brown Esq.
All rights reserved

ISBN: 9780986092855

TABLE OF CONTENTS

Chapter 1	TWINTRODUCTION	5
Chapter 2	THE TWIN CODE	7
Chapter 3	TWINSANITY	14
Chapter 4	TWINANIGANS	23
Chapter 5	COTWINCIDENCE	35
Chapter 6	TWINSPIRATION	45

Acknowledgments   57

Chapter 1 – TWINTRODUCTION

It seems people have always been fascinated by twins. Even twins are fascinated by other twins. I myself admit to getting curious, fascinated and intrigued when I bump into other twins. I hit them with the same barrage of questions that my sister and I get – Are you all twins?! Who's the oldest? How many minutes apart? They give me the same stare that I sometimes give others who seem a bit too overenthusiastic (like a stalker who's way too close). They relax though, when I tell them I'm also a twin and we start chatting about all things twin.

Suffice it to say, there's just something about that TWOness, that prenatal partnership, that amazes folks. It's not that hard to figure out why. Afterall, according to twinsfoundation.com in 2014, twins represented only 2% of the population in the United States, which amounts to approximately just 4.5 million twin individuals. Just imagine how much smaller the percentage seems worldwide. It's definitely a relatively small and infrequent occurrence. What can I say? It's a TWINOMENON!

Most people easily recognize identical twins because they are identical in appearance. However fraternal twins are not as easily discernible, and are not given as much focus and attention. No, it's true. Do we fraternals resent this? Of course, we do! No shade to our identical twin counterparts, but we think identical twins are way overrated. Yup, and this is where I come in.

Now, I don't plan on getting into the monozygotic or dizygotic scientific details (although our scientific names sound pretty cool, right), but I will try to be as crystal clear as possible in fleshing out the special circumstances and situations we fraternals encounter and endure on a daily basis.

Reactions when encountering fraternals may vary, but the same comments are usually made. Some will note that we look a lot alike and could be twins. Others say, "There are two of you?!" Some will even say that we don't look alike at all. Every now and then, we get an unusual comment – one woman walking behind my sister and I said to us, "You all must be twins, because you walk exactly alike!" That was a little different and left us chuckling, but we usually get the standard remarks.

One thing that happens with us, and other fraternals I'm sure, is that people will linger longer to examine us closely, to point out both the similarities and the differences between us. They try to see if they missed something when they first noticed us. Once they realize that we are really twins, they want to know if we are like identical twins. Can you trick people? Did you ever switch classes? Are you all very close?

Well, allow me to unravel some of the mystery that is the Twindom in general, and the Fraternal Twindom specifically...

Chapter 2 – THE TWIN CODE

Let me warn you at the outset, that you will probably get very tired of my made-up twin terminology, but I simply cannot help myself. I must admit that I have always had way too much fun being a twin. Waaay too much fun. So, sue me! Many of us really do get a kick out of the doubletakes, and most of the questions or the stares of disbelief, confusion or amusement.

The first thing I need you to understand is that there is a code of conduct under which most twins operate. After all, this twindom doesn't just happen all willy nilly (I've been waiting 3 books to use that phrase). On the contrary, twins operate under a somewhat predictable code of conduct. We don't take oaths (well, anymore – I believe that practice ceased in the early 1300s). However, the code has been standardized and placed into an official, codified "TWIN CODE". The Code is periodically updated as new twissues arise, but the basic rules and expectations remain the same.

I'm not really sure how identicals operate, but the most important aspect of THE TWIN CODE for fraternals is birth order. It is extremely significant and there is no such thing as overemphasis of this point. It stands to reason that the twin who makes it out of the womb (or birth canal) first, must always be given deference and the utmost respect from the secondborn twin. Was it not the somewhat pushy and bossy secondborn who kicked us out of the womb and made us the opening act, so to speak, because they were too afraid to explore and take the lead?

This is simple logic or common sense, and is covered in the first chapter of the Code, in three different sections I might add. When you're an identical, and look exactly the same, it matters not who was born first. There's a clonedom of sorts, going on and they have more pressing matters to deal with. Fraternals, however must establish order inwardly first, before facing a judgmental world that prefers identicals. Yup.

I have actually witnessed situations in which a secondborn has completely taken over the twindom, essentially rendering the firstborn mute and it is one of the most heartbreaking realities to behold in the twin world. Just deplorable (you heard me). I implore firstborns who find themselves in this unenviable position, to reclaim their birthright. Assume the lead again, before twinsanity ensues. Sure, we are a team, but right is right! Don't be fooled. It doesn't matter if a mere four minutes separates the two of you. There are levels to this thing. Order must be established and maintained or fraternals as a unit will be ignored completely.

Some of the mandates in the TWIN CODE are for the parents of twins. Believe it or not, not all parents of twins get it. They can really botch the job at the outset if they're not careful. How? Well, one way is by getting the twin names all messed up. Fraternals are already fighting an uphill battle. Why then, I ask, would parents not try to help out by coming up with appropriate twin names? I mean, we may not look exactly the same, but it helps to have cutesy, creative or rhyming type names when trying to convince an identicals-happy world that we really are twins. Am I right? Why is that so hard? Was the labor that difficult that naming was no longer a priority? I mean, let's be honest – real talk, many of you had a Caesarian. The naming should have been finalized long before the third trimester.

I may sound a little bitter, but hear me out. My sister and I have names that begin with the letter 'A'. That's nice and they get a little credit, but NO. Anita and Audrey. There's no rhyme. There's no harmony in pronunciation. One has two syllables and the other, three. It might ease the sting a bit if we were named after other relatives, but there were no other Anitas or Audreys three generations back and eventually I stopped looking! I ask questions, but people abruptly change the subject or walk away. To alleviate the anguish, I have recently come up with Nee and Dree, but it hurts. It really hurts. Don't do this to your twins. It's wrong and more importantly, it's in violation of the TWIN CODE.

Another serious parental obligation outlined in the TWIN CODE is the duty of the parent(s) or guardians to NEVER allow the school system to separate their twins based on twin status alone. It is so nonsensical to worry that fraternals will not develop separate personalities if they are in the same classes or classroom. It is even ridiculous to assume this will happen with identicals. Despite having been wombmates, we will develop distinct likes, dislikes and personality traits. Will we be close, have a special bond and support one another to the utmost? Certainly! But knock it off with this 'separate the twindom' practice. It doesn't work and in some cases, the separation can lead to the exact thing they were trying to avoid.

I recall they tried to separate my sister and I as early as pre-K school. The Head Start program was held at different parks in our town. For a few weeks, we were having fun, minding our own business, making progress (yes, at 3 and 4) and making friends. Then all of a sudden, some genius decided they should send Audrey to a park program clear across town. Not only is this a twinconvenience for the parent (in our case, my maternal grandmother who shared our birth date and raised us did not have a car...and even if she did!), but it's based on faulty logic. I think our separation lasted all of two days, because Audrey pitched a FIT at the other park. On the third day, we were reunited and it felt so good. Take THAT!

The bottom line is that it was a stupid practice. I hope they don't do it anymore. If it has been observed that the twins are exceedingly dependent upon their twin to their detriment (which is poppycock), that's one thing. However, other things can be done to ensure proper personality development and independence without imposing traumatic separations so early in life. My twin and I were in the same classrooms on and off throughout our school years (same K, 4th, 6th classrooms and same 9th and 12th grade homeroom) and we turned out okay. We are TWINSEPARABLE!

    One last TWIN CODE provision I will mention (because there are far too many to cover them all) is one that all twins are guilty of overlooking from time to time. My sister and I have often called one another up during the day to say, "I don't believe I've heard from you today, and it's almost 4 o'clock". This is a clear violation of Chapter 9, paragraph 1, Section 7 which states that twins are to contact their wombmate no later than 2pm EST, EVERY day. I suppose this is not a top priority for identicals since they can 'feel' one another (whatever), but it is of paramount importance for fraternals. The only exceptions or excuses allowed for violating this portion of the TWIN CODE are coma and death.

There will be another sub-provision to this particular rule in the 2017 edition of the TWIN CODE that says, at the close of each day, wombmates must call, text or facetime the other, 'GOODNIGHT'. My sister and I have already had this covered for the past 7 years or more. If I do not hear from her by 10a.m. the next day, I am notifying the police, the FBI and certified twin psychics (I know identicals don't need that last thing, but we don't care about those showoffs).

Let me end this chapter by saying that violation of these rules, codes and mandates is no small matter. It is very serious indeed. We are duty-bound to uphold these tenets of the twindom as laid out in the TWIN CODE. Furthermore, even though snitching on your twin in other normal circumstances is generally frowned upon, blatant violations and utter disregard of the rules must be brought to the attention of the appropriate enforcement officials. This involves a Board that is voted in, you guessed it, every two years. (It's all about the TWO). Twinfoolery on a large scale will Not be tolerated. In my Captain Kirk voice, THERE WILL BE REPURCUSSIONS!

Chapter 3 – TWINSANITY

Aside from the chaos that can result if Code rules are violated, there is a certain amount of wackiness, weirdness and sheer twinsanity that simply comes with the territory. For example, why are twin parents hell bent on dressing their twins exactly alike? We are fraternals, for crying out loud. TWINSEPARABLE. We do our own thing, maaan. I bet even identicals aren't thrilled with being dressed the same. After that whole need to separate the twins so they can develop distinct identities thing, what sense does it make to dress us exactly alike? (although I must admit, I actually think it's kinda cute, even for adult twins, but I'm trying to make a point here, so please try to follow me).

We are not robots. We (fraternals) are not clones. We like different colors and different styles. Sometimes we feel like those poor pets dressed up against their will for holidays and special occasions, for the amusement of their owners and handlers. It ain't right! Did it ever occur to these addicts of outfit assimilation that one twin might look fine in bright orange, while the other sticks out like a sore thumb? A bright orange thumb! Of course it never occurred to them. Nor do they care. At this point, it's all about the parents' need to draw the oohs and aahs and relive their childhood, dressing vicariously through their innocent twins. Sigh. It's actually quite shameful, considering some of them are the ones who couldn't even come up with creative names, but are now all of a sudden, creative fashionistas. Twinsanity!

Another inevitability that fraternals must deal with is the notion that even though we are not identical, we should be a lot more alike than many find us. Ummm. NO! How many times do we hear, "You're so much taller than her!" or "You're so much thinner than her!" Etc. etc. Just because we hung out in the womb for about 9 months, doesn't mean we're coming out the same height, weight, complexion and whatnot. I don't even think identicals come out exactly the same in every aspect. Use these differences to your advantage, so you can maybe figure out which twin you're talking to. Use some sense, common or uncommon. The ignorance is unsettling.

Sadly, common sense and sometimes even common courtesy go out the window when people talk before they think. My sister and I have actually had people say to us, "Which one is the smart twin?" or "You're the one that's not married, right?" or "Your sister is beautiful. Y'all aren't identical, right?" I mean, they will actually say these things to you with a straight face. One asked me, "Why aren't you married yet? How come you don't have any kids like your sister?" Yeah, we encounter some real winners at times.

Now don't get me wrong. There are some clear distinctions between twiblings. The twin package deal is exactly that – a deal, an arrangement. One twin gets certain attributes and characteristics in the twin package, and the other gets others. For example, there is usually a cutesy, dainty twin and one who is more athletic and tomboyish. I'm sure male twins have their twin package split also. There is usually a taller and shorter twin, and a thinner and bigger twin. Audrey is the tall, thin one and the gorgeous, head turner. I am the not so tall, not so thin one who can't be bothered with makeup and nails and such. She is the serious, no-nonsense type, while I am the silly, always up to something type (nothing bad, mind you...no really).

Controversy always ensues when the question is asked (and people do ask), "Who's the mean twin?" I will state unequivocally that my sister is the mean twin (but if she asks, I will deny I said it). Most twins will deny being the mean one and feign niceness, but don't be fooled. Well actually, you can't be fooled. Sooner or later, it will come out and you will know who the mean one is. Audrey really isn't that mean (well, it depends on who you ask – don't ask her daughter), but between the two of us, she has less patience. Now if a twin tells you outright that they are the mean twin, run, RUN like the wind!

Despite the fact that we are twinseparable fraternals, twinsanity still abounds. For example, even though Audrey is the taller, thinner twin who wears her hair straight, and I am the shorter, average-sized twin who wears her hair natural or braided, people still call Audrey, Anita (or Nita) and call me, Audrey. Whether or not we bother to correct them depends on the day, the mood, the full moon or the direction of the wind. It's much easier to just go with the flow and let them call you whatever they want (within reason). Apparently one twin name resonates more with some and that's the name they're going with no matter who they're talking to. It makes no sense to yell, "I'm ANITA! Not Audrey" because this will quickly get you labeled as the mean twin.

   I myself have actually resorted to saving time when I address other twins, by simply calling the person Twin Twin. My sister's coworker used to call me that and it makes sense now. You don't have to remember names, because they are both a twin and everybody's happy. I even have folks online and at Audrey's job calling us Twin Twin now. Others just say 'Hi, Audrey's sister' or 'Hi Miss Brown's sister'. Listen, when I'm tired or trying to save time, even I call Aud, Twin Twin, so it's all good.

   Another crazy thing with us is that we both work in fields (in the same town) where we have encountered a lot of people over the years (she works in a hospital and I am a teacher). I bump into her coworkers or clients/patients and they stare at me as if they know me, or will tell me something, thinking I am her. A lot of my former students and teaching colleagues will go to her job for tests or to visit sick relatives, and stare and ask her, "Do you have a twin sister named Miss Brown who is a teacher?" Hilarious. I often have to remind myself not to get aggravated if someone stares at me unusually long because it could be a former student or it could be someone that thinks I'm Audrey. You get used to it and eventually learn not to take any of this wrong name stuff personally.

There's another kind of twinsanity that comes with the twindom, but it borders more on the dumb, than the twin if you get my drift. I mean, there are actually aspiring rocket scientists out there who will ask 'When is your birthday?' and in the next breath ask my sister, 'When is yours?' I'm talking about people who know we're twins. Others will ask if we have the same father. Now, there are some strange, scientific possibilities where fraternal twins can actually have a different father, but SERIOUSLY?! I am both amazed and worried that these people are allowed to wander the streets on their own. It's not right.

Some dolts actually remark, "How can you be the older twin if you both have the same exact birthday?" Two things. Maybe three. One, you rarely get the chance to use the word 'dolt' but I think it's perfect for this scenario. Two, I take greater offense to minimizing the importance of birth order, than I do to being called the wrong name on purpose. It's in the CODE for crying out loud! If you must know, I don't even like when folks say, 'Hey Audrey and Anita'. NO, it's Anita and Audrey. YES, in that order, dagnabit! What is the sense of going through all that trouble to crawl out from the safety of the womb into this mysterious new world first, if you're going to be disrespected like that. It's TWINSANITY!

And another thing. Why on earth would you tell a twin that you don't like their twin? Who does that? You'd be surprised. They don't out and out say, I can't stand your twin but the signs are there. I mean, we're all adults, and not everyone is going to like everyone else, so we should be mature about this, but NOPE! Some information should be kept to yourself. It is what it is. It's petty and juvenile, but it's a universal truth. You don't like my twin? You're dead to me. Muerto! And that's the TWUTH!

    Probably the most twinsane thing about being a wombmate is the undeniable power of the twindom. Gospel legend Sandra Crouch alluded to it when eulogizing her twin brother, the legendary Andrae Crouch. There is an overwhelming sense of the need to protect your twin from anything, big or small. Individually, in school I felt I could take any teasing from some pretty lame, loser-types that wanted to be popular (and as long as they didn't get physical, I got through it).

    It's one thing to endure bullying or wrongful treatment yourself, but to witness your twin being teased, or somehow wronged, ignites a unique kind of rage. I suppose it's similar for other close folks, but for me, it's all-consuming and bothers me to an extreme, volatile level. It can be the simplest slight that might not even bother my twin, but WoohooWEE! Anyway, I think most people understand that, and are smart enough not to approach twins at the same time if they have bad intentions. However, some tried it.

When we were in elementary school, my twin was hospitalized with asthma every year, and I could always count on some cowardly punk to try something because they knew I was by myself. Luckily, it never got out of hand and I never really bothered my twin with the details. But talk about a cowardly move. I'm embarrassed For them!

Anyway, believe it or not, I think the over-protectiveness has gotten even greater as we age. For example, there are times that I just cannot be at my sister's job and hear how some indignant or impatient folks get loud, rude or hostile (at least that's how I take it) with her, because even though it's all part of working with people and she knows how to quell those situations, and can more than fend for herself, I take it all Very personally. I really do. I know. I need help. I'm working on it, but hmmmph!

Anyway, hopefully folks get this and act accordingly. But if ANYONE has a notion that they can bring harm to my sister, I assure you my wrath and rage will be formidable, and I'm not even the mean twin.

Chapter 4 – TWINANIGANS

I don't want this to take a sinister, or twinister turn but I have to get to one of the uniquely odd predicaments that fraternals sometimes find themselves in. First of all, we are regularly pressured to Prove, on the spot, that we really are twins. Strangers and acquaintances alike, will say to you, "Y'all not twins! No, you're not!", to which we maturely respond, "YES WE AAAARE!" That's not enough, though.

The doubters want proof! What are we supposed to do? Carry around birth certificates, notarized letters and our drivers license? Don't think they don't ask to see these things either. As I mentioned before some ask us both when we were born. I guess they're trying to trip us up, make us nervous and hoping we'll confess saying, "Okay, you got us; we're not really twins." But who would make up being a twin? And why??? Boggles the mind!

Another thing. I know I said that birth order was extremely important. Well, some might think birth order is probably irrelevant in terms of wishing a twin Happy Birthday, but not so fast.

Why on earth would you wish my secondborn twin Happy Birthday before me? How dare you! I don't even care if you don't know me, and only know Audrey. Right is right. Ask questions. Find out. Secondborns resent this and try to get revenge by not acknowledging your birthday greeting until their actual birth time has arrived. Yeah, they try to pull birth time on you, because it's their only real weapon or power in this twindom.

At least, that's what my secondborn tries to do. She can be quite unreasonable. If it's not 7:44 a.m. she will say, "It's not my birthday yet!" Can you believe it? Who does that? Then she has the nerve to sleep past the birth times anyway, not only missing wishing me Happy Birthday first at 7:40 a.m. as she is duty bound to do, but cheating me out of my chance to say Happy Birthday to her at the time she insists upon. She goes too far!

Some other twinanigans that arise are due to no fault of our own (and occur mainly because of inadequate filing systems and record-keeping). I have been to medical offices that pulled up my sister's chart, because the person looked for it according to last name-first initial or birthdate, instead of by the number the chart was assigned, probably to avoid just this kind of mixup. This happened mainly before my sister married and became a hyphenated, but even a couple of times afterwards. Because we live in the same town, and frequent some of the same establishments, it can become a problem. We've had issues at voting polls, accountants' offices, pharmacies and the like.

Speaking of hyphenated names and marriage, courting, dating and such, it is RARE that a twin will immediately, if ever, truly like their twin's choice of date, mate or spouse. Nope. It just doesn't happen. It is a clear invasion of the twindom. Believe you me, the intruding 'applicant' undergoes a thorough vetting by their would-be twin-law. It is a brutal, vicious, hostile and admittedly unfair process. I mean, frankly, what qualifies Anyone to step in and try to claim your twinseparable, with whom you have shared a womb and with whom you've spent virtually all of your life as a team, save a few minutes at birth? For the life of me, I can't think of a single qualifying factor. Sure, the applicant may love your twin unconditionally and worship the ground he or she walks on, but so what! No one can love a twin more than their twin! Period! NOPE!

As for me, let me be completely honest. NO ONE will EVER be good enough for my twin. I mean, no shade to my brother-in-law, but the facts are the facts. She is a gem, and no one can measure up. Sorry. And it doesn't help his cause AT ALL that he is an identical twin! I mean, talk about a betrayal. I've since forgiven her but it wasn't easy. True story, when I first noticed her future husband sniffing around, I said to her, "Who is that clown?!" Well, how was I supposed to know she was seeing him? He often teases me about crying hysterically at their wedding, but I assure you those tears were not for the reasons he's thinking. Lemme stop. Suffice it say, fraternizing with identical twinanigans are tough to overcome. I am happy to report that I am almost to the point of acceptance. Almost but, well, never mind.

I guess spousal acceptance of one's twin is a bit difficult because, contrary to popular belief, twins don't usually like the same types. I could be going on and on about some real 'catch' and bursting at the seams, infatuated and then I'll show my sister a picture or introduce her to the hottie and she'll be like, "Yeah, he's okay". And vice versa. It may seem petty and stubborn, but it is simply the way it works. What floats her boat, sinks mine with the quickness. Clothes, shoes? Yes. Men? No. This is probably the case with most twins, or maybe I am the mean twin afterall?

I recently read about identical twin sisters who were not only dating the same type of guy, but it was THE SAME GUY! To make matters worse, they did it on purpose, because they said they wanted to be identical in every way. They had plastic surgery to continue looking identical. They wanted to be pregnant at the same time, by the same man and even more bizarre, they slept in the same bed together with this man at night. Those twinanigans are too weird and kinda creepy!

That, of course, is an extreme case and I'm not saying this might be another example of the shortcomings of being an identical twin, but this would never happen with fraternals. I'm just saying. Okay, let me stop teasing my identical twin counterparts. I love all twins. I just wanted to emphasize that it is rare that twins like the same type of partner. Let me move on...

At some point in the womb, a determination has to be made about who will get what in the twin package. GOD does the bulk of this work, but we do barter amongst ourselves. As I mentioned earlier, you have the short and tall twin, the dainty and tomboy twin, the athletic and maybe bookworm twin, the nicer and the meaner twin, the party twin and the loner twin. One twin might be laidback, while the other is more easily rattled or the hotheaded, tell it like it is type. One may underthink things, while the other overthinks things. Luckily, the twin attributes are usually distributed evenly enough and a sort of checks and balances dynamic makes this whole twin package thing work. There is however, one aspect of this distribution of attributes that can lend itself to twinanigans...

There is always one twin who most will agree is the sneaky one. The one you have to watch. The one that always seems to be up to something.

Not necessarily something bad, but just busy planning and plotting, well, fun. That twin usually has a mischievous twinkle in their eye or an impish grin (as my Nana used to call it) that is a telltale sign they're about to engage in some sort of foolishness or tomfoolery, for which the other twin has little patience.

As you may have guessed by now, I am that twin. If you check our earlier photos, you will note the eye twinkle and the little grin. Sometimes, I'm not even up to anything, but because of those traits, people think otherwise. I would take great umbrage at this assumption, were it not true that 9 times out of 10, I AM up to something. I can't help it. You will often hear the mischievous twin saying, "What???" Yup, guilty.

To my twin's credit, she is a trooper. She is the reel it in twin. I am the out on a limb twin. I can't help but to get into stuff and situations. I plan stuff and come up with some really wacky things for my twin to cosign. I have her going on ill-advised treks with little notice, getting me out of hair-issue jams and all manner of ridiculousness. Forced her to endure my different musical obsessions with Frank Sinatra, John Legend and Bebe Winans, to name a few. Good thing she loves me so much, because I don't even know myself why I do half the things I do. In my defense, how can it be my fault if it was all decided in the womb? I like to think we hashed it all out in there and agreed on it before we touched down, so why complain now? Am I right? Whenever I innocently say, "What?", in response to her accusatory expression and tone, she gives me 'the look'. I'm sure we're not the only twins that go through this, so please come out of the shadows to validate these twinanigans.

There are some really sensitive situations that can give rise to twinanigans as well. One involves your twin naming his or her children. Now, if you and your twin were not blessed with adequate, appropriate or adorable twin names, it is incumbent upon the twin who has children first to make up for this egregious affront (you heard me) to the twindom. It is an open wound that must be healed in the next generation. It is covered explicitly, exclusively, extensively (and by other 'e...ly' type words) in the 8th chapter of the Twin Code. Yup...

There is of course, no guarantee that a twin will have twins, which would make things so much easier. However, let me use my sister's and my situation to explain what I mean. When I first learned that my sister and her hubby were expecting, I was excited and hoping for a nephew, because we have a lot of females in our family. I wasn't even thinking of a name, to be honest. After testing, they were informed of a possibility of serious health issues, and had to get second opinions and more tests. The tests would not only confirm or rule out risks, but the gender would be revealed as well. When she told me that she would be naming the child after me, if it was a girl, I could care less about her having a boy. Come onnn down, Girl! Even though the birth was scary, because my niece was a preemie baby, born two and a half months premature, and weighing only 1 pound, 14 ounces, what a blessing she is to our family some 19 years later.

What's her name? Well, this is where the twinanigans comes in. I admit that I was not yet that familiar with all of the tenets of The Twin Code (even though I was in my early 30s then), but I later learned that not only was I right to feel honored to have another niece named after me (my brother and wife gave their first born my middle name, Andrea Marie), but it was my sister's duty to bestow that honor upon me, according to Chapter 8, Section 2, paragraph 3 of the Code. And I quote, "...It is the duty of the birthing twin to make their firstborn child a namesake of their twin..." Yep, it's all there in black and white. Although I never had any children of my own, I had planned to have a twin son and daughter (yes, had it all worked out) and was going to name them Audrey and Aubrey (I can still adopt, so stay tuned, but I digress)...

There was a slight twist however, in the naming of my twiece (niece by twin). She did name her daughter Anita, after me, just like she said. Only thing is, Anita is her middle name. I mean, who am I to argue about first name vs. middle name? There are other relatives to consider on both sides and she may have always had a name in mind. So what name knocked Anita into second place? CHANEL. That's right. She named my niece after her favorite perfume, Chanel No. 5. She dropped the 5 part of course, but HUH?!!!

How does one's twin twin, wombmate, soulmate, sole mate in the womb come in 2nd place to a perfume made by a Russian, French chemist? We're not even Russian or French! Eventually, because the kid was so cute, I let it go. By the way, you do a lot of letting go as a twin, lemme tell ya. I amuse myself by dubbing our aunty-niecy relationship as Big Nita & Little Nita. Suffice it to say, naming twinanigans can cause irreparable harm amongst twinseparables if not handled correctly. I've seen it happen. Yup. Thank God I'm the bigger person. I could have bought an official case before the High Twin Court.

The other touchy issue I mentioned involves a twin getting married. It is assumed by twins and non-twins alike that a twin will automatically select their twin as the maid/maiden of honor or best man. It is afterall, in Chapter Five of The Twin Code. A very serious matter indeed. This was never an issue with my sister and I. We are extremely close and have never even had a physical fight in our life. I wasn't thrilled with the color scheme she selected but as I say, twins let a lot of things go for the sake of the twindom.

I would be lying if I said I wasn't astonished by the fact that some twins, fraternals and identicals, are just not that close. There have been instances where a twin actually tried to kill their twin, or frame them for a crime and then there are twins who have had knockdown, drag out (showing my age here) fights. Who does that? It must be weird when identicals physically fight each other, because it's like you're punching yourself. I can't.

Despite these cases where the twin bond is not as strong and the closeness not as apparent, I still have to believe that when the not-so-close twins select someone other than their twin as their bestman/maid or maiden of honor, the other twin deep down is really hurt by that. Yes, we twins have our own best friends etc but selecting someone else for arguably the most important day of your life, goes against all things twin. I don't care what ya say. It is a violation! Soon, there will be twins that don't bother to include their twin in their wedding at all, or in any of their significant life accomplishments and achievements. That's when I'm heading straight to the high court. Just Wrong. Twinanigans!

Chapter 5 – COTWINCIDENCE

Fraternals do not usually have that psychic, telepathic ability to feel physically or emotionally whatever the other twin is feeling even if not in the same place. Nope. We have no "twintuition" like those overrated identical celebrity twins to whom my sister and I are always compared. (Teehee, just kidding; we love T & T). Fraternals do, however, have our fair share of what I like to call cotwincidences. These are strange, odd things that seem to happen for no other reason than being a twin. Let me explain...

My sister and I have opposite body types. She is tall and thin, wears smaller sizes and has longer legs and arms so we don't usually have the same options when it comes to clothing styles. I am shorter and not so thin. That dressing twins the same thing is easier when younger, but because of our different sizes and body types, we rarely dress the same as adults. It's hard to find the same style in our different sizes. Actually, we rarely dressed identically when we were young either, because we were pretty poor growing up and my grandmother (NANA) concentrated more on practicality, durability and affordability than matching outfits. I mean we didn't have hand-me-downs. We had hand-me-overs, meaning you wear it today and I'll wear it tomorrow. Got teased a lot for that, but I digress...

Despite our different body types and style preferences, I can't tell you how many times I have shown up at my sister's job (or to her house, or when meeting for an outing) and discovered that we were wearing the same exact color scheme. Sometimes, just the top and other times, the same color pants and top, or footwear. This is clearly cotwincidence. We do wear the same shoe size and borrow each other's footwear, but we usually don't buy the same shoes.

The most delightful example of this happened when we attended my niece's high school graduation. My sister was running late and came straight from work. She had on her black work pants and jacket with a pastel yellow top. I had on pastel yellow pants and a black top. I thought that was so cute and poignant - sending off 'our' little graduate wearing the same colors. Her husband swore we planned it even though we didn't (identicals are so jealous; teehee, haters).

Another cotwincidence is how the child of one twin can look so much like their twaunt or twuncle that folks believe the aunt/uncle is actually the parent. That happens a lot in our twindom. My twin's coworkers often remark that Chanel looks more like me than her mother. I can be out with my niece and people will ask if she's my daughter. When I tell them no, they give me an "I don't believe you" look as if someone would lie and say their child isn't theirs. People are nuts!

When I say, "No, really. I'm not her mom; she's my twin sister's child", they then give me that slow, knowing headnod, like they've experienced a profound revelation. They seem to be utterly amazed at the twenetics. It is kinda weird though, because in some pictures, she looks like her mother's minime, or little clone (awww) and in other pictures, she looks a lot like me. It's eerie, but in a cool beans sorta way. We call her our triplet, because sometimes when all three of us are together, people actually call us that. My sister has a coworker who is a fraternal twin and the same is true of she, and her niece. Sheer cotwincidence.

I am actually happy that my twin and I don't get that 'I feel sick when the other feels sick' thingy. Don't get me wrong - When my sister is ill, I am very sad because I hate to see her even the slightest bit uncomfortable or sick or injured, but being able to Feel that physically, and regularly, must be torturous at times. It would make me miserable more often than not.

In our twin package, I got all the food allergies. She has only 3 to my 30 or more, so it was ironic that she wound up in the E.R. once after an allergic reaction to some nuts she didn't know were in her food. I almost had a breakdown (I'm also the wimpy twin). I lose it if she even has a fever, for crying out loud, so that literally feeling each other's pain thing wouldn't be good.

We did have a coinkydink thingy once though, in unexpected, back-to-back emergency room visits. We didn't plan it, didn't want it, and don't even like emergency rooms like that (even though Aud works in a hospital ER sometimes) and yet, stuff happens. Audrey was at work one day, and her pressure shot up sky high because she had an allergic reaction to something in her office. She was in the E.R. for hours. She was discharged late at night and I had to drive her home, because her husband was unavailable at the time. Did I mention that I'm not the twin who responds well in emergencies? I panic, and driving while stressing or emotional is not a good thing for either of us – somehow, by the grace of God, we made it home.

You've probably noticed that I'm also the longwinded twin (the habitual digressor) while Audrey gets straight to the point. Anyway, I was trying to say, that just a few days after Aud's unexpected emergency room visit, I wound up in the E.R. after feeling faint and lightheaded, and breaking out into a cold sweat. Turns out it was just dehydration, but it was just odd how that happened in the same week. Some of the E.R. staff, our friends and family joked that I just wanted attention and to be like Audrey and that's why I wound up in the E.R. Put away your copycat conspiracy theories. This kinda thing just happens with both fraternal and identical twinseparables. Just cotwincidence is all.

We've only really had a handful of whoa type events in our 50-year plus twindom. One time, we wound up getting the same, exact birthday card for one another. It was funny because we lived on different sides of town and shopped at different stores. She gave me my card in an envelope and when I handed her hers, she asked why was I giving her the card back. That's when I opened up the envelope and realized it was the same exact card. It wasn't even a twin-specific card; just a lovey-dovey sister type deal. I couldn't tell you now to save my life what was on the card, because we don't freak out or get sappy (well, we do get sappy and say awww a lot) about that kinda thing, but it was a pretty cool cotwincidence that made everyone laugh and say wow.

One time we actually did have the closest thing to twintuition as you can have as a fraternal I suppose. I was walking down the street and could smell fire, see smoke and hear fire trucks. I can't explain it but I just felt a weird, overwhelming sense of dread and fear, and was almost in tears. Before I even had a chance to call Aud, she called me and told me there had been a big fire in the building where she worked. Turns out she wasn't in the building at the time, but that feeling that danger had befallen my twin was not a good feeling at all.

    I would not want to experience that regularly, close or not! I know when she's sick, or upset, or something's not right and that's enough. Again, we have this agreement to end each day with a call or text to say goodnight, love you. I told her hubby, if anything weird happens to her, or she is missing, I will know and I am coming for him first, so he better have a damn good alibi or I'm going straight to the police. I know. I'm SO wrong and biased against the identicals. I'm working on it though.

    Speaking of being suspicious, I recall an incident that still leaves a bitter taste in the mouth of my beautiful wombmate. We were in the same history class once in high school. I was the nerdy twin who really dug history, while Aud could pretty much take it or leave it. For some reason, our teacher decided to put us on opposing sides of a debate. I have to say, we were pretty evenly matched and offered compelling arguments for our positions. Welp, I decided to go for the old, end-all, debate strategy. Aud was claiming something that was counter to the statistics I was relying on. Sooo, I countered her argument with a phrase that haunts me (and her) to this day. I said "Statistics show they do" and that was enough to win the debate.

When I tell you Audrey was mad? (Remember we never had those "I'm not speaking to you" type arguments that lasted more than minutes even. Never!) Well, after the debate, she wouldn't even talk to me or make eye contact with me. We shared a locker and she uttered nary a word. I offered up the lame, 'Hey no hard feelings' line and she was having none of it. Got to the point of saying to our friends, "Tell Anita, I'm not speaking to her" even though we were standing right near each other. Oh, it was UGLY!

I say all this to say, THIS was no mere cotwincidence. This was a twinspiracy! Pitting twins against each other is low, LOW on the totem pole of human interaction. It is wrong. It is sadistic. It is hateful, unnatural and unnecessary. It just isn't done. This kind of thing can cause scars so deep, they may never heal. We can laugh about it today (well, not really and I suggest you never utter the word 'statistics' around Aud), but for a while there, the twindom was on the verge of...gulp...emotional and physical separation. Anyhoo, I got an A in history that year, but we never speak of the debate. Well actually, I do bring it up every now and then just to aggravate her (remember, I'm That twin. Teehee).

There is one more thing I want to share that also borders more on the twinspiracy side than cotwincidence. You be the judge. I had just graduated law school and was interviewing for potential attorney positions. One interview was for a federal job in D.C. but the interview was to be in Philadelphia. My sister and my boyfriend at the time were both working, so she had her boyfriend drive me there.

Now anyone who knows me, knows I'm a huge Washington Redskins football fan and had dragged my sis, her boyfriend, my cousin and numerous others, countless times to games and other football events in D.C. Therefore, we had been on highways enough times to find our way to Philadelphia. Well, somehow we got lost. Very lost! We wound up in Freehold, NJ – yes Bruce Springsteen's hometown (Jersey plug. Sorry).

Finding our way back to I-95 was an adventure and needless to say, I missed the interview and my relocation to D.C. never happened (which wound up being a good thing, since it turned out that teaching was my real calling). For years, I had chalked it up to a 'not meant to be' type thing, but as I thought about it more, I wondered if me not separating geographically from my wombmate was really the result of some sort of twinspiracy. Could she have told her boyfriend to get lost on purpose? Hmmm? Okay probably not, but it's fun to say that to her. Teehee.

Chapter 6 – TWINSPIRATION

If you take nothing else from this book, let it be that we are indeed twinseparable. You can separate the two of us and find that we have distinct personalities, gifts, desires, dreams, passions, fears, strengths and weaknesses. We really don't mind being referred to as the twins, as long as you realize there are two of us. Two, separate individuals who happen to be twins. Yet, it is also true that we are inseparable and that twinspiration is at the root of mostly everything we do.

We constantly think about our twin. Or is that just me? Perhaps I need a few more hobbies. Anyway, we see a good show or movie. We call the twin. We hear a funny joke. We call the twin. We discover a new, tasty food. We call the twin. We forget something. We call the twin. Both simple and serious decisions always involve consulting our wombmates. If you are moving, how far? Will it be easy for me to get there? Maybe we should get Facetime. Getting married. Having a baby. Buying a car. Gotta have twinput. It's a given.

Even though, we are individuals, we are still essentially twinseparable. Yes, we have separate lives and different BFFs and friend circles, but we can't go too long without touching base. When one goes on a trip for a day, a weekend or longer, there is an uneasy feeling that stays there until we know the twin has returned.

I honestly don't know how twins make it living in separate states, thousands of miles away. I mean I'm a mature adult and I know life happens and opportunities, marriages etc. beckon us elsewhere, but I can't fathom living states away from my twin. I would have to plan to see her in person at least once a month, or every other weekend. Nope, I'm not going anywhere. Maybe that's just us though, and not all twins. Could we possibly be Too Close like they warned of in our preschool years? NAH! We are both independent and twindependent, and that's fine.

Both fraternals and identicals have what I like to call twinpathy. We understand life as a twin, so we just love other twins. As I mentioned before, even twins get excited when they see other twins in their travels. We usually have excellent twadar and can spot fraternal twins quicker than most. Sometimes, our twadar fails (very rare) and we may not feel one way or another about someone, until we find out they're a twin. Well, that changes everything.

Yes, we are biased. It becomes a 'well, why didn't you say you were a twin?' type thing. We pull out pictures like new mothers, and exchange funny twin stories. And I pity the fool that says something against a fellow twin. Excuse me? Whatchu NOT gonna do (pardon my slang) is call a twin out his/her name on my watch! Nope! Unless of course, it is my twin that has a beef with your twin, then all bets are off and forget that twinpathy crap – Whatchu say to my twin?!

I probably shouldn't say this, but each twin has selected 'their twin' of other twin sets. Yup, they won't say it out loud, but just as is the case with nontwins, we are saying to ourselves, "Yeah, Twin A is my favorite". Or Twin B, das my Twin! I even have a favorite Mowry twin and I don't even know them. It's so wrong, yet there you have it. Please don't ask me to reveal my faves if you happen to be one of the twins I know, because that could get very awkward, and I never want to hurt another twin's feelings.

Twinpathy also involves a very special combination of sympathy and empathy. Of course, we sympathize with some of the negative growing pains all twins face (i.e. the good twin, bad twin type labeling). This can be a serious issue as even some twin parents unknowingly or knowingly show a preference for one twin (even if they're identical). One twin can be deemed better, or more this or more that than the other and trust me, twins are bothered by this like any other siblings. It can lead to longterm insecurities and fracture the family dynamic. Try to avoid this twin labeling with the twins you know. Makes a world of difference.

The saddest part of twinpathy, however is the empathy we feel for any twin who has lost their wombmate to heaven. I say empathize, because although we can imagine the pain and despair that comes with such a profound loss, no twin can truly know or even really wants to know the depth of that heart wound. To lose your other half, your better half, your heart, is unthinkable and yet it happens.

   We had 5 sets of twins in our high school graduating class and 3 twins have experienced the loss of their wombmate. In one case, both twins have passed on. We cannot know that pain and yet we feel a special kinship with our brothers and sisters in twin. We care and worry about them, so we check up on them. We once had a neighbor who was a twin and we didn't know it until he told us one day he was celebrating his birthday for the first time in decades (it was his 50th). Then he told us the reason why was because he stopped celebrating his birthday in his 20s when his twin sister died. We just hugged him and we all cried. It is unwritten and yet understood that although we can never replace their twin, we're going to adopt them into our own twindoms until they reunite with their wombmates in heaven.

   It may seem like I'm off track in talking about twinpathy, because I was supposed to be talking about twinspiration. However, the truth of the matter is that twinpathy is a major part of what inspires me. It is also true that my biggest twinspiration and inspiration in my life now is my sister. How can I explain it?

Okay, the person who has had and continues to have the single most impact in and on my life and the way I live it, is my beloved, maternal grandmother (Hazel Smith), who raised us. She is now my Angel. Again, Audrey and I were born on her 52nd birthday. When we lost her in 2005, it was hard – still is – and it was the most profound loss I'd ever experienced. Yet, I still had twin twin to help me through. If I had lost my twin instead, not even my sweet NANA could have provided real solace. That is how special being a twin is.

I joke about my twin twin, Audrey Hazel being the mean twin, but in all honesty she is a sweetheart (and I'm even over that whole thing about her getting my Nana's name as her middle name, instead of me). Seriously though, she inspires me like no other. She is so beautiful, strong, loyal, loving, dedicated and selfless (sometimes to my utter aggravation, because she deserves the world in my not so humble opinion) and I just hope her husband and daughter appreciate that. I'm sure they do, but I'm just saying. These are the kind of things that keep me up at night. Yup, that need to protect.

People don't believe we can be as close as we claim to be. They get sick of us saying 'our' and 'we' all the time. Some will even say "Oh brother" if they witness an example of our closeness, because they think it is fake and exaggerated. On the contrary, it is very real. Case in point, she once demonstrated a twinpathetic act that I will never be able to repay. When I was in middle school and so self-conscious about having short hair because I was teased mercilessly about it, I wore a scarf every day to cover my head. Some days, kids would snatch the scarf off my head to further tease, intimidate and humiliate me.

Well, my twin had hair that grew more regularly, and longer. Yet throughout that time, she chose to wear a scarf on her head every day too, in solidarity. I will never forget that, and it brings tears even now as I type it. Her unique understanding of my fears, my pain and her sharing in my joy, and vice versa is the essence of our twindom and I'm sure many other twindoms.

She Gets me. She Knows me. She has my back, unconditionally.

Sometimes, we discuss how things are to go when one of us ultimately passes on. Ideally, it would be the same day. I have explained to her that if I go first, she must notify my dearest online friends, have a closed casket, and a pantsuit (no dress) etc. She tells me, she'll be too distraught to do any of that and the casket will remain open so she can see me. She also told me to help her write what she's going to say now, because she'll be too distraught to think (I got the writing skills in the twin package, but does she really think I'm gonna write my own eulogy for her? I think she's serious). Anyway, I can see she's gonna be difficult and I'm working on a backup person to carry out my wishes. She says she is sure I will give her a wonderful eulogy and I tell her, "I don't know what you're talking about; I'm going with you". Yep, I will be jumping right into the grave with her, and no one can stop me.

Maybe a less morbid anecdote will better shed light on our twindom. It turns out a woman I worked with, was a distant relative and she relayed a story that always makes me chuckle. She said my twin and I were very young at the time, and were in the back seat of a car she was riding in as a passenger. She said she had to turn around because she heard the strangest little noises. Apparently, Audrey and I were chatting and she said she couldn't figure out what we were saying, because we were talking so very fast and incoherently that it sounded like a foreign language to her. She said she couldn't even make out the words we were speaking, but that we were giggling and happy. And there you have it. We Were speaking another language. The language of twins. It is undecipherable to all other ears, but ours.

Suffice it to say, we and most twins really enjoy being twins. We're gonna ride this twin thing until the wheels fall off, so I need the haters to get over it. Like other twins I'm sure, we still parade each other around to our clients, parents, coworkers or friends, saying "This is my twin. Doesn't she look like me?" We pretend like we hate it and roll our eyes, saying, "Will you stop with the show and tell", but WE LOVE IT! It is the coolest of beans.

What's really cute is when someone says they want to be our twin, or they say to someone else, "I'm their twin." We actually do have some honorary twins, but I won't name names because some people might feel some kinda way if they're left out. I'm not really going to get into how some of my sister's coworkers favor her slightly and others, therefore take it upon themselves to call that person Audrey's twin. I don't mind because I know they're just playing around. Well, actually I do mind it, and that kinda thing is forbidden by The Twin Code, but I'll let it go - for now.

In closing, the bond that exists between most twins (whether sisters, brothers, brother and sister, fraternals or identical) is unparalleled and there really aren't adequate words to truly convey the depth of that bond and how very unique it is, although I have tried. We complete each other. You have the same thoughts, and complete each other's sentences. My sister and I even say the same exact thing at the same time, in one voice in response to something/someone we're watching or some strange thing we've seen. We always LOL when that happens.

We are two separate people who do have our own BFFs, close relatives, love interests, spouses, children etc. with whom we are close. Yet, there is only one person with whom we have shared a womb for at least nine months of Pure TWOness. Except for a few minutes, we have never been alone in this world, and that's pretty special.

Well, I think I'll end this twiopic right here. After all, I can't give away ALL of the secrets of the twindom. I've already said TWO much as it is. We fraternals have to remain TWINCOGNITO because the infidels are circling. The anti-fraternals are out there. Oh, what a tangled wombmate web we weave, when first we practice to multiply (mul-ti-plee) conceive. Don't ask me why I said that last part, as it's completely irrelevant to the point I was trying to make. These things just pop into my head and I feel compelled to share them. (Yes, I'm That twin also). Anyway, you now know everything you need to know about Club Two, Team Twin and Wombmate Warriors. On behalf of myself and all TWINSEPARABLES, Carry On...

ACKNOWLEDGMENTS

I must first acknowledge my Lord and Savior JESUS CHRIST. Through HIM all things are possible. Through HIM, I have received this gift of writing.

I also acknowledge my READERS - all those who have read this and my other two books. It is difficult enough to put your thoughts on paper for all to see, without worrying about how it will be perceived and received, but the fact that people take the time out to read my work is something I will always treasure, and something I will always be humbled by and grateful for.

Eternal Love for THE BEST TWIN SISTER anyone could ever have – my better half, my Stistuh, my Wombmate2, my Four Minutes, my Heart, AUDREY HAZEL BROWN-GIVENS. I was our opening act, and she closes out the show. She is simply TWAAAWESOME!!!

Shoutout to my niece CHANEL ANITA (Lil Nita).

I must also acknowledge our older brother MELVIN BROWN, Jr. because we're a Trio (THE BROWN KIDS). NOD to my UNCLE BOBBY & 1st cousin, JUDITH COMPTON II, who is also like our triplet and Of Course, our parents CAROLYN & the Late MELVIN BROWN, Sr. Twins LOVE twin parents because most rock and, let's face it, they did all the really hard work to bring us here. SMILE.

Shoutout to all the twins in my family (I believe Audrey & I are the oldest) – then there's BONITA & BONNIE, KEILAN & KELVIN and MAX & CHRIS. Then there's ANTONIO & ANTHONY (brother-in-law) and Aud's brother-in-law DERRICK & DEBRA (a). Derrick's twin Debra passed away in the womb and the small 'a' represents ANGEL twin.

Shoutout to the Fab 5, the five sets of twins in the 1983 graduating class of Clifford J. Scott High School in East Orange, NJ – Anita & Audrey, ROBERT & ROBIN, TIONE(a) & SHANNA, CHRIS (a) & MIKE and GILBERT (a) & GLENN (a).

Shoutout also to our middle school classmates, sisters MARVA & MARSHA.

I really know a lot more twins than I thought. Next I want to acknowledge my neighbor twins. Shout out to twin sisters KIM & KAREN and their younger twin brothers WAYNE & SHAWN.

Shoutout also to twins DARRIN & DARRYL, KEITH & KYLE (a), TRACEY & STACEY, TRACY H & her Angel Twin (a) and next generation neighbor twins of another Anita, KELLY & KENNY.

Then there are DIANE & DONNA, SHERYL & SHARON, and VANESSA & VALERIE, my sister's coworker twins.

I definitely have to shout out my former twin students. Sister and brother, JESSICA & JESSE, and four other sets of student twin sisters MIA & MERCEDES, RACHEL & MELISSA, TINA & DINA and SHANNIKE & SHANIELLE.

I've even met twins online. Shoutout to dear twinnie friend PHYLLIS (a) & her HARRIET (a), CHRISTINE KAY & her MARGUERITE FAY (a) and to identical youngin twins JESSICA & MEGAN.

As far as celebrities, no shade to the Mowry identicals, but my favorite well-known twins are CARVIN & MARVIN WINANS. Tragically, LOL, the Winans twins are an example of a twindom where the Secondborn (Marvin) has assumed the role of the Firstborn (Carvin). I don't know if it's with Carvin's blessing or if he simply has no choice.

I may as well acknowledge here that as much as I remind Aud that I am the Firstborn, and she is not the boss of me, she really IS the boss of me. I don't wanna get on her bad side. Nozzur. If she calls and says, be ready at 1:30 and hangs up, I'm ready at 1:30! HEY, it is what it is, maaan.

Because this is getting long, I want to end by just thanking ALL OF MY FAMILY & FRIENDS for their support & encouragement. Means a lot! And if I left any twins out, it's probably because I don't like yawl. I'm KIDDING! I'm a Kidder! No shade intended & apologies in advance for any omissions, misspelled names or mistakes in birth order (perish the thought, but work with me people - I'm on a deadline here!).

Last but not least, I must always acknowledge, remember and THANK my sweet grandmother, HAZEL CHARLOTTE ROY-SMITH. Although my beautiful angel NANA was not an actual twin, we were her birthdate twinnies. I will forever declare my eternal gratitude and LOVE for her because she made me the woman I am today. I don't owe her anything. I OWE HER EVERYTHING!

www.ingramcontent.com/pod-product-compliance
Lightning Source LLC
Chambersburg PA
CBHW061514040426
42450CB00008B/1610